How-To-Draw,
Paint, & Craft
with your creative
Grandkids

These projects are recommended for children 8 and above. Grandparents, always carefully supervise your grandchildren when enjoying these activities together, especially around water, in the kitchen, or when using sharp objects. Remember that any activity involving small parts can present a choking hazard and is not suitable for children under the age of 3. Before beginning any activity, take into consideration your grandchildren's ages, abilities, and any allergies they may have, and adapt your plans accordingly. Be sure to check product labels and to buy child safe paints, clay, and other materials. Read labels carefully and follow instructions. Stay safe and have fun!

How-To-Draw, Paint, & Craft with your creative Grandkids
ISBN 978-1-7331603-3-9
Published by Product Concept Mfg., Inc., 2175 N. Academy Circle #201, Colorado Springs, CO 80909
©2019 Product Concept Mfg., Inc. All rights reserved.
Written and Compiled by Patricia Mitchell with other contributing writers in association with Product Concept Mfg., Inc.

You don't have to be an artist, or even think of yourself as "creative," to enjoy these fun projects with your grandchildren. With only a few basic supplies, you and the grands can go from drawing pictures to mixing clay, from putting together a collage to carving personalized stamps. You'll even find a section on hand lettering. The section titles use fun lettering styles that are provided right in the book.

Step-by-step instructions are included, and, throughout the book, you'll find idea-starters designed to spark ideas and inspire creativity. And even more important is the shared laughter, conversations, and good times... and the memories to last forever!

ARTS & CRAFTS BOX

A box of basic supplies is your go-to place when grandkids come to visit! All you need to do is bring it out, put it on the table, pull up some chairs, and let ideas and creativity flow. Though you may want to tailor the contents to their ages and interests, here's a general idea:

- A variety of paper colors and weights – include plain printer paper, card stock, construction paper, tissue paper, tracing paper
- White and black foam core
- Various paints – tempera, watercolor, craft paint, acrylics (note that acrylic paint is not washable – cover clothing and work surfaces when working with it)

- Mat board
- Colored pencils
- Pens, glitter pens, markers, crayons
- Brushes
- Scissors
- Glue
- Tape (regular and double-sided)
- String, yarn, ribbon
- Dried flowers

There are some needs for specific projects, but these items are things you probably have around the house or in the yard, or can be found at any craft store.

All you need is a plain box with a lid. If there are young children, delight them by covering a plain box with gift wrap or novelty fabric that reflects their favorite superheroes. Older children may enjoy decorating their own box. Solve substantial age-gaps by creating a box for each group. Embellishments and add-ons might include:

- Greeting cards, with scenes or designs cut out
- Photos or pictures reflecting child's interests
- Shells
- Fabric
- Ribbon, yarn, string, ric-rac, trim
- Stickers

From now on, no more worries about one of those surprise visits...or how to keep them entertained on a rainy day!

Make a box like this to store finished projects, too! or for flat artwork make a portfolio with two pieces of heavy cardboard taped together on one long side so it opens like a book. Store in a closet or lay flat under a bed.

This lettering style is Ladybug.

See all the fun lettering styles you can learn starting on page 56.

Ready...Set...Draw

You'll find all kinds of drawing exercises in this section. If they seem advanced for your grandchild's age, you can simplify. Having fun with creative expressions is the most important thing. We'll start with step-by-step instructions for drawing animals.

HUMMINGBIRD

Two ovals, one large and one small... and two cones, one large and one small... are all you need for head, body, and wings!

A dot makes an eye... now add a beak and tail.

Add shading and sketch in a few little details, and your hummingbird is ready to fly!

4

PANDA

Start with different sized ovals and circles.

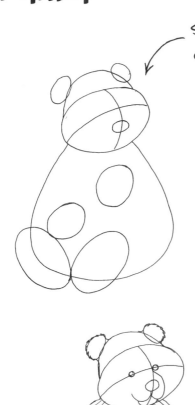

Lightly draw guidelines across the face for eye- and mouth placement.

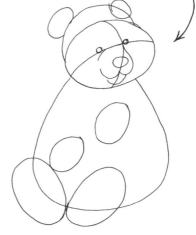

Continue with the arms and legs.

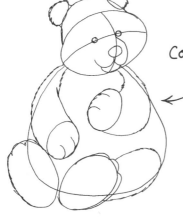

Add shading and sketch in the details that make your panda your own!

BUNNY

Start with circles and ovals!

Small sketched lines make the bunny soft and furry...

and add final little details.

COUGAR

Start with circles and ovals!

sketch in details...

lots of little lines are all it takes to create definition and fur.

ROSE

Draw a small oval and then draw a small heart around the oval. Add two small petals to the bottom and draw another heart around everything. Add a curved petal below.

Connect heart to curved petal. Begin adding petals, gradually making them larger.

Continue adding petals alternating left and right. Draw a curved line to form bottom of rose. Add three leaves.

Add details and a stem!

DOODLE BUTTERFLIES

Design and doodle these butterflies in your own way!

Fine line markers are fun to use to make detailed line work.
Or color in with colored pencils and markers. You can trace
around cookie cutters and other objects to give grandkids
other shapes to doodle
and design.

DOODLE BUTTERFLIES

You can also doodle around shapes for a fun look!

HOW TO DRAW CARTOON ANIMALS

You can follow these steps to draw any kind of animal you want to!

Start a sketch with a few simple shapes,...

...refine your line work to define eyes, ears, mouth,...

...continue to add details!

A horn turns the horse into a unicorn.

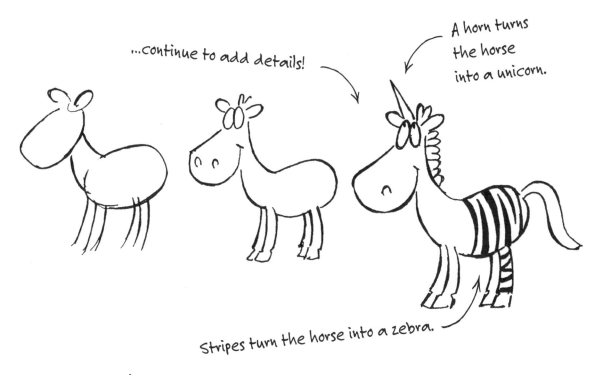

Stripes turn the horse into a zebra.

Jump right in to draw a silly frog!

Or just monkey around with any animal you like!

Use these animal ideas for starters - then draw your own fantasy critter that only you can imagine and create!

CARTOON CHARACTERS

Below are some ideas to get you started with your very own cartoon people.

Start with one of these shapes for a head, or make up one of your own.

What feeling do you want to give your character?
Happy or sad? Silly or serious? Goofy or sweet? Add
eyes to give your character expression!

fear

angry

goofy

"whatever"

surprised

sorrow

Noses come in all shapes and sizes!
Here are a few ideas...
what else can you think of?

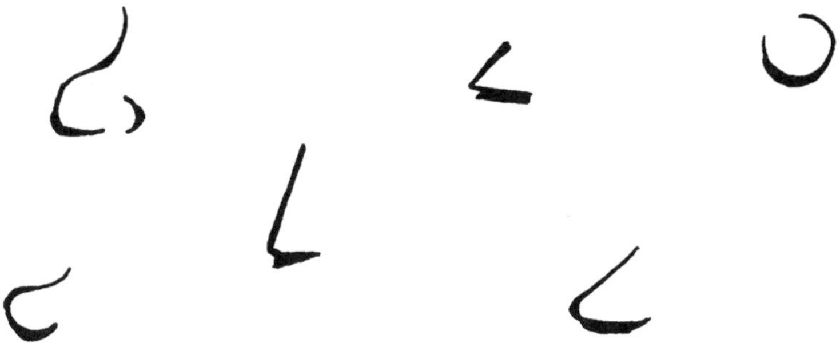

The mouth "says it all"...have fun with one of these, or use your imagination to come up with something different!

Add a body...hair...clothes...shoes...accessories... and maybe you'll want to draw some friends to keep your character company!

ROBOTS ARE SUPER COOL!

By combining various shapes, you can build a robot!

Start with a head...what shape do you think it should be?

Add a body.
Square?
Cylindrical?
All kinds of shapes put together?

How does your robot get around?

Be creative and add arms...legs...feet...
antennae...gears...dials...what else can
you think of that would move your robot
way into the next century?

Use your imagination to build a
spaceship, castle, pirate ship,
or anything you can imagine!

AMAZING FACE FACTS!

These amazing facts about the human face will give the kids a kick. Try out each of these theories by testing them out on each other, or by looking in the mirror (you can use a ruler, but measuring with the thumb and index finger work just fine). It's wild how often these face facts are true, no matter our age differences! *(except for babies...they haven't grown into their heads yet).*

FOR KIDS (AND GRANDPARENTS!) WHO LIKE TO DRAW, THESE GUIDELINES CAN MAKE A BIG DIFFERENCE IN YOUR NEXT DRAWING!

WHERE IS THE TRUE MIDDLE OF THE FACE? Measure from the very top of the head to the bottom of the chin. Right in the middle of that space is where your eyes are! Yes, almost always, the bridge of the nose, between the eyes, will be the middle marker.

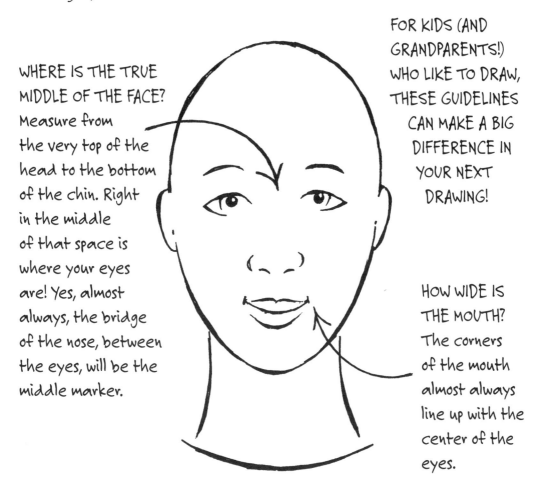

HOW WIDE IS THE MOUTH? The corners of the mouth almost always line up with the center of the eyes.

WHAT'S THE DISTANCE BETWEEN THE EYES?
Turns out that almost always it's the same width as one eye.

WHAT'S THE
DISTANCE BETWEEN
THE TOP OF THE
EYES TO THE
BOTTOM OF
THE NOSE?
It's one and one half the
width of the eye.

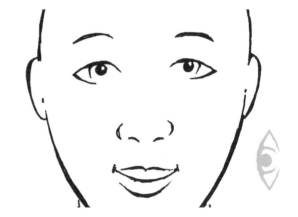

WHAT'S THE DISTANCE
BETWEEN THE NOSE AND
THE BOTTOM LIP?
You guessed it, one eye.

WHAT ABOUT THE WIDTH OF THE NOSE?
The distance from one side of the nostril to the other is again,
one eye width.

BODY FACTS!

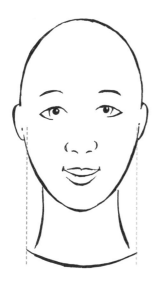

AND HERE IS HOW YOU FIND OUT HOW WIDE THE NECK IS. So often we think of a skinny little neck holding our heads up. It is actually thicker and stronger than you would normally think. Find the point where the bottom of the ear connects to the jaw. Now run your fingers down to where the neck connects to the shoulder. You will probably find that point is almost the same width as the space from ear to ear.

THE HEAD TRICK!

Stand against a wall and check out this theory: An average human's height is seven times the height of his or her head (except for very young children). See how many times this fact is true for the grandkids.

HELP YOUR GRANDKIDS LEARN ABOUT ANGLES WITH THIS "HANDY" TRICK.

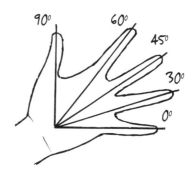

A NEW WAY TO DRAW TREES

If you ask a young child to draw a tree, it will typically be a simple shape like this, sort of like a lolly pop just standing on top of the ground.

Take a walk with the grands and help them see in a whole new way how trees grow. Look at each part of the tree as it grows and notice how the tree limbs literally branch off into a V shape. There are thicker branches on the lower part, but each branch grows out into another V...and each of those branches into another V...and each of those...Well, you get the idea, the branches get narrower and narrower, smaller and smaller all the way to the top.

Now help your child see how many times they can keep branching out into more and more v's in their new drawing of a more realistic, living tree.

This lettering style is Giggle.

Build & Sculpt

Children will enjoy the hands-on experience of working with clay, paper maché, foil, cards and cardboard. Let imaginations soar!

BUILD IT WITH CLAY

Many child safe brands and kinds of clay are available in craft and hobby stores. Polymer clay, a popular choice, works for various projects. After kneading a lump, it softens and becomes a versatile sculpting medium. Even if you take your time molding, polymer clay will remain malleable. It will harden as it bakes in the oven. (Grandma should supervise when using the oven.)

Air-dry clay is also easy and fun to work with. Unlike a polymer clay, however, it hardens as it dries, so there is no need for baking.

You can find both clays in a range of colors.

Or, you and the grandkids can mix up your own clay with ingredients right in your kitchen!

There are several ways to make clay using only flour or cornstarch, baking soda, and water. Food coloring is optional. Two recipes are printed here, but many more can be found online.

Recipe 1

1 cup cornstarch
2 cups baking soda
1-1/2 cups cold water
Food coloring (optional)

Mix all ingredients together in a saucepan over low heat, stir until a dough forms. Remove from heat and cover with a damp towel, allowing it to cool before use.

Recipe 2

4 cups flour
1 cup salt
1-1/2 cups water
Food coloring (optional)

Mix all ingredients together in a bowl to make the clay. Sculpt, then bake sculpted pieces on a non-stick cookie sheet for about an hour at 350°. Place on a wire rack to cool.

Clay pieces can be decorated using acrylics, tempera paints, poster paint, or nail polish. (Note: acrylic paints are not washable, so cover clothing and work surfaces when working with it.) Store leftover clay in a tightly sealed jar or follow directions carefully if using purchased clay so it stays moist and usable.

On the following pages, you'll find a range of fun and easy clay projects. Or, you might want to hand each of the grand-kids an unformed lump of clay and see where their imaginations take them! For projects calling for a flat slab of clay you can either flatten by pressing with hands, or use a rolling pin.

- For some clays, it may help to cover clay with waxed paper before rolling out. (Make sure to remind young children that clay is not edible.)

- Don't use grandma's best baking rolling pin...use an inexpensive rolling pin, empty plastic jar, etc.

CLAY GECKO

You can make all kinds of animals, both real and imaginary, using the technique shown below.

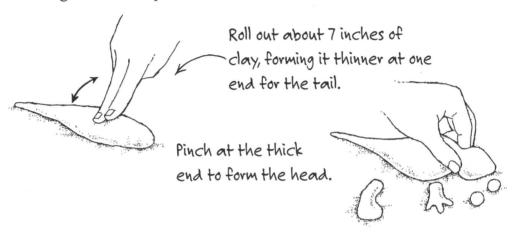

Roll out about 7 inches of clay, forming it thinner at one end for the tail.

Pinch at the thick end to form the head.

Roll out shorter lengths of clay for feet and toes. Attach limbs using the score and slip method: With a fork, make small holes in each of the pieces to be joined. Wet a dab of unused clay and press it between the two pieces. Let dry completely.

Make eyes by rolling two small balls of clay, attach to head and use a pencil point to press eyeballs..., or press in two cloves or peppercorns. Add texture to damp clay with a pencil tip, fork, or other object.

When clay has hardened and is completely dry, decorate your gecko with a colorful painted design! What other critters can you create?

CLAY JAR

Gather a selection of items that will make interesting impressions in the clay: shells, buttons, coins, fork, pencil eraser, the tip of a wooden spoon.

What can you find in your junk drawer? A toy car makes a cool track!

Roll out a 12" x 4" clay slab, about ¼" thick. While the clay is still damp, press items into the clay then remove and see the cool textures they create!.

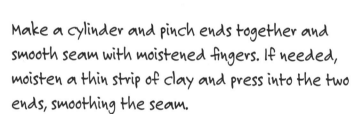

Make a cylinder and pinch ends together and smooth seam with moistened fingers. If needed, moisten a thin strip of clay and press into the two ends, smoothing the seam.

Prepare another clay slab for the base. Set your jar on it and cut around, attaching cylinder to base by pressing and smoothing the seam with moistened fingers. If needed, moisten a thin strip of clay and press between sides and bottom, smoothing as you go along.

CLAY PLAQUE

Make a personalized plaque to show school or team pride, mark an achievement, or simply to celebrate you!

Have ready a picture of school or team mascot, emblem, or other element, along with texturizing tools, such as a fork, butter knife, spoon, paper clip, etc. You'll also need a pencil, straw, or other tool to make a hole for hanging.

Roll out two rectangles of clay, one smaller, one larger, about ¼" thick.

Texturize around the larger slab to make a frame.

Place the smaller rectangle on top, gently pressing the two slabs together.

Now, using a pencil tip or other tool, add name, words, symbols, and other items. Use the eraser end of a pencil or a straw to make a hole for hanging. When clay has hardened and is completely dry, add paint for color and design.

CLAY ROSE

With a series of circles and a couple of leaves, you can create a perfect rose!

Roll out a thin sheet of clay.

Cut 10-15 graduating circles going from approximately 1/2" to 2". (You could use coins, bottle caps, etc to use as guides for circle shapes)

2 inches

Half inch

Overlap the clay circles, starting with the smallest and ending with largest.

With moistened fingers, carefully roll the circles starting with the smallest and ending with largest. Fan out to form petals.

Cut out a couple of leaf shapes to form a base.

Gently press into shape, and let dry. Shade with touches of paint...spray tips with glitter...make a whole bouquet!

PAPER MACHE

Paper mache consists of layered strips of newspaper and thick glue molded around a foundation form. For a foundation form, you can use wire, crumpled newspaper, foam shapes, cardboard, paper towel tubes, or other items. For the glue, you can either use a pre-made mix found in hobby stores or a simple mixture of two parts flour and 3 parts water, which the kids can stir up till it's a nice glue-like texture. (Adjust as needed. Add more flour if too thin, or more water if too thick.) Your creation will harden as it dries. It can take days to dry out, so prepare a project space that's out of the way and cover your surface with a disposable tablecloth or trash bags.

For your paper mache creation, you will need:

- A bowl of glue mixture, whatever you choose from the options above

- 1" wide strips of newspaper in various lengths, plus lots of extra newspaper for forming shapes.(Tip: If your sculpture will be light in color, use paper towel strips for the final layer so the newspaper print doesn't show through.)

- Bendable wire, such as a thin metal clothes hanger

- Masking tape

- Add-ons to fuel the imagination: feathers, foam, paint, pipe cleaners, straws...you get the idea

Get started!

You might encourage kids to make sketches of their ideas first, then choose their favorite design. What stirs the imagination? A castle? Person? Animal? See the next pages for ideas!

Spread your work surface with a covering. Bend wire to form the starting base. Wad, roll, and twist newspaper around wire base to form the shapes needed and wrap tape around and around. Build up areas as needed until the form is complete. Other forms to use could be cardboard, or foam. When the basic shape is formed, cover it with paper mache. Lay a paper strip in the glue. Have your grandchild run two fingers down the strip to remove excess glue back into the bowl. (If paper is too glue-laden, it will take a long time to dry.) Keep layering and building the desired shape. When the form has taken shape, let it dry out completely before going to the painting and decorating stage. Use craft paints and markers, and let dry. Now bring out the glue, glitter, and fun to finish the creation!

Create supersized wild and whimsical bugs!

After forming the body with wire, crumpled paper and masking tape, secure antenna, pipe cleaner legs, and form wings out of wire. You can cover wire oval wings with either paper mache or see-through colored cellophane, with details in marker. If you want to hang your bug from the ceiling, be sure to work in a wire loop to add string to. Paint sculpture with fun shapes and colors, then glue on all kinds of fun features: eye balls, fuzzy brows, etc. The only place you'll find more creative bugs is in Nature herself!

What scientific name do you want to give your insect?

- You can make a worm like this by making the foundation from 5-7 foam balls glued together.

- Make a fun and imaginative animal! For this llama, a woven fabric scrap is used for the blanket, and little fabric pieces glued on. Yarn can be added for reins. What animal would you like to create? Look for pictures to follow and sketch out your ideas, then brainstorm together creative ways that can make them come to life.

- Make an athlete, astronaut, dancer, drummer, or cartoon character! This ballerina has a light paper mache covering over the wire form. Form the tutu out of a circle of heavy paperboard that is held up by toothpicks or crumpled paper while the paper mache dries and hardens. What could you add? Glitter to her outfit? A ribbon around her waist? A flower or feather in her hair?

BUILD IT WITH CARDS & CARDBOARD

Everything from a deck of cards to pieces of cardboard to paper towel tubes figure in to these projects! Building possibilities are endless, and guaranteed to keep the grandkids busy for hours. Here are a few ideas to suggest to the builders.

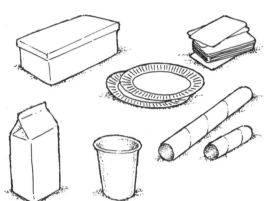

CARD TOWER

Here's a use for a set of inexpensive playing cards, or an incomplete deck...

...or a stack of 3 x 5 cards, painted with your own geometric patterns and designs for a really cool look.

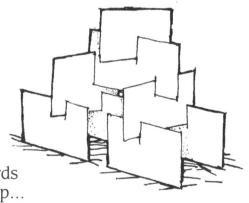

On the sides of each card, snip about ¼" in...

...that way, you can insert cards in any creative way to build up...

...or out...

...or any which way.

PAPER TOWN

Take a walk in the neighborhood and notice the shapes of buildings, doors, windows, roofs and chimneys.

At home, cut out a variety of shapes – circles and half-circles, squares, triangles, rectangles – out of colors of construction paper. Supply a large piece of paper and glue. Invite the grand-kids to arrange the shapes to create a neighborhood.

PLAN A CITY

Calling all young engineering minds! How would you design your own city, using yogurt cartons, jar lids, colored paper and a little creativity? These urban projects could go on for days, so find a place to store it. Or, simplify so it's just a project for several hours. Make your own box shapes, or use boxes from around the house such as package deliveries, milk cartons, tissue boxes, paper towel rolls, all painted or covered with construction paper.

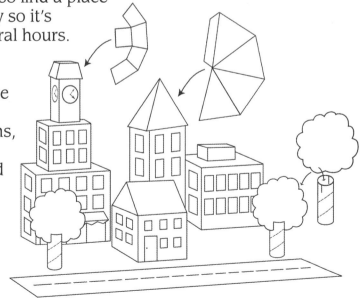

DOLLHOUSE

Build a basic house with a cardboard box. Securely tape pieces of cardboard on to make a second story, and to make a roof. Add strips of paper or paint tile or shingles for the roof.

Make furniture from small scraps of cardboard and glue them together.

 Create a stove from a small box, color on a window and burners with a pen.

Make a small cup of paper or use a bottle cap and cut-out small flowers from colored paper.

 Create a rug with your own pattern and cut the ends to make fringe.

Create a couch by folding cardboard then gluing on end pieces, draw lines for cushions.

Make a desk out of some cardboard pieces glued together.

When your house is about finished, you can paint the outside as siding or bricks, use cut fabric for curtains or rugs, cover walls with gift wrap, wall paper scraps, or contact paper, or paint your own design.

A tiny plastic bottle with a jar lid on top makes a table. Use an upside down cupcake liner for a table cloth! An upturned mini cupcake liner is a lampshade when you place it on a straw or pencil. Keep your lamp steady by placing it in molding clay, styrofoam or maybe a marshmallow! Can you think of other ways to make a unique house? Think outside the "box"!

PAPER PLATE FLOWERS

Use a stack of paper plates, or cut circles out of construction paper for this project.

Cut four paper plates or circles into flower petal shapes, each plate's petals a little smaller than the last.

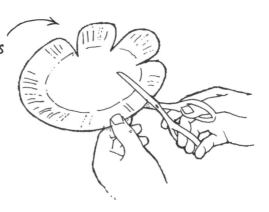

Glue the center of the plates together, one on top of the other. The largest plate goes on the bottom, and smallest on top.

Curl the petals, using either fingers or roll around a pencil to achieve desired flair.

For the center, use a marker or paper punch-outs from colored paper to make small dots...glue on a button...add a sticker...what do you think?

Paint in brilliant colors, or leave white as an elegant alternative.

SWIRLY CURLY BUTTERFLIES

Paper towel or toilet paper cores are excellent for this project. Or make tubes out of construction paper or light-weight cardboard. Along with scissors, glue, crayons or markers, and maybe glitter pens and pipe cleaners, you're all set to create swirly curly butterflies.

Start with a tube made out of construction paper, or use a paper towel core, or a toilet paper core. Cut tube into 1/2" circles.

For the wings, pinch one end of four circles and glue them together.

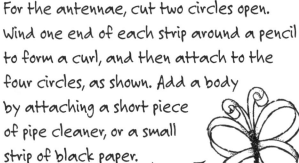

For the antennae, cut two circles open. Wind one end of each strip around a pencil to form a curl, and then attach to the four circles, as shown. Add a body by attaching a short piece of pipe cleaner, or a small strip of black paper.

Create a wall hanging by adding your butterflies to stem made out of circles and a few strips curled at the end. Arrange, embellish, and decorate as desired!

BUILD IT WITH FOIL

Keep an inexpensive roll of foil on hand and you'll always be prepared for a simple, spontaneous sculpture session! Cut square pieces of foil to scrunch or roll up for the bodies, and give kids different lengths and widths of foil to twist into arms, legs, heads, and tails. Pipe cleaners are a nice addition for necks, ears, and even antennae!

What else can you make? animals, athletes, dancers, aliens, a fancy tiara, a funny hat…

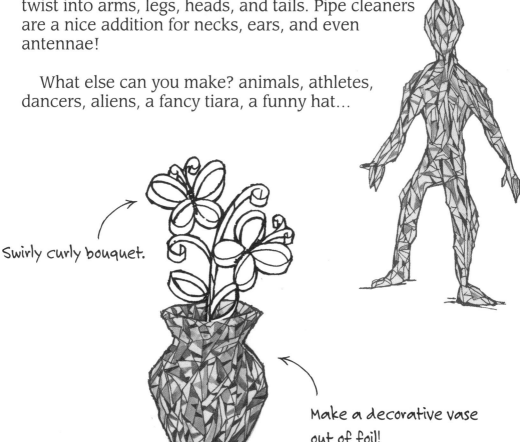

Swirly curly bouquet.

Make a decorative vase out of foil!

CARDBOARD BOX DIORAMA

Create a dimensional scene that the kids have an interest in: a rocket ship landing on the moon with a starry backdrop, farm with a barn and animals, castle or fort with bridges and secret hideaways, or an animal habitat. Here's an example:

Bear Habitat

Start with a shoebox. The lid becomes the floor, and the box, laid on its side, forms the shell.

Line the lid with a thin piece of polystyrene foam covered with leafy-patterned or camo fabric or paper.

Mold the bear out of air dry clay, then paint.

Make a tree using a colored or covered paper towel roll for the trunk.

Make branches out of brown rolled construction paper, twigs or pencils and attach to the tree.

Add a bird's nest made out of raffia. (Roll raffia around fingertip, then move the "nest" off and dot with clear glue, or set in a bottle cap to rest and keep its form.)

Scatter bits of raffia on the "ground".

Collect stones and place a few in your diorama as boulders.

Foodie Sculptures

This lettering style is Easy Peasy.

Your kids will have great creative fun exploring how different fruits and vegetables look like characters, animals, flowers, and all kinds of things – with a little artistic help. If they grocery shop with you, let the kids look through the produce for items that inspire them. What face do you see in a green pepper? What shape does a yam remind you of? And what are those dance moves the little chilies seem to be doing?

Then help them create their vision! You will need to do the cutting for them using a small knife, following their directions. Common items that might be helpful additions are toothpicks, cloves, raisins, carrot and celery pieces, etc.

ALIEN APPLE

- Green apple
- Blueberries
- Grapes
- Cloves
- Frosting Tube
- Toothpicks

Cut chunks of apple to create shape of alien.
Toothpicks topped with blueberries make antennae.
Add cloves to grapes for eyes, and attach with toothpicks.
Draw a mouth with frosting tube.

INCH WORM

- Celery
- Cream cheese
- Cherry tomatoes, grapes, or olives
- Peppercorns
- Toothpicks

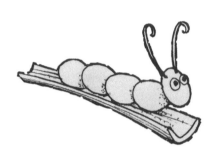

On a piece of celery, put 5-7 cherry tomatoes, grapes, or olives. Use small pieces of toothpicks to hold them together.

Make eyes with two dabs of cream cheese and two peppercorns.

Cut a toothpick in half to form antennae...how beautiful you are!

OWL

- Apple
- Orange
- Lettuce
- Radish
- Cloves
- Carrot
- Toothpicks

Cut an apple with a flat base to match a flat cut in an orange for the body. Apple slices make the wings and tail, lettuce pieces for the ear "feathers", an olive or cream cheese with a raisin in the center for the eyes. More cloves create a pattern on the chest.

MERRY MOUSE

- Kiwi fruit
- Strawberry or apple slices
- Black olive
- Cloves
- Red licorice lace or celery stalk
- Toothpicks

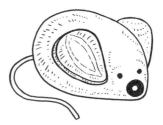

Make a small cut in the kiwi fruit so it has a flat base. The tapered end of the kiwi forms the mouse's head. With pieces of toothpicks, attach strawberry or apple slices for ears. Attach a black olive for a nose and cloves for the eyes. Add a length of licorice lace or string from a celery stalk for a tail. How easy...and how cute!

PERKY PENGUIN

- Eggplant
- Blueberries
- Carrot
- Red pepper
- Toothpicks

Remove a slice from the eggplant to form the penguin's vest. Use the cut slice to make flippers and tail. With small pieces of toothpicks, attach blueberries for eyes. Make a beak with the tapered end of a carrot. Form feet with two carrot chunks or slices.

SILLY SQUASH ALIEN

- Yellow squash
- Grapes and cloves, or cream cheese and peppercorns
- Cherry tomato, blueberry, or grapes
- Radish
- Blueberries (optional)
- Raisins (optional)
- Frosting Tube (optional)
- Toothpicks

Make a small cut on the wide end of the squash so it stands upright. For eyes, use small pieces of toothpicks to attach grapes, or insert cloves, or use a ball of cream cheese and peppercorns. Attach a cherry tomato, grape, or blueberry for the nose. Attach a radish slice for a mouth, carving teeth, as desired. Use toothpicks for arms, forming "hands" with grapes or blueberries. Decorate with raisins or blueberries, attaching with dabs of cream cheese or frosting tube.

LIME TURTLE

- Lime
- Grape or cherry tomato
- Carrot
- Cloves or peppercorns
- Frosting Tube

A lime is the body for the turtle, cut to have a flat bottom. Designs can be cut into the "shell" to form a pattern. For the head use a grape or cherry tomato, carrot chunks cut for the neck, tail and legs. Use cloves or peppercorns for eyes, draw mouth with frosting tube.

BEAUTIFUL BUTTERFLY

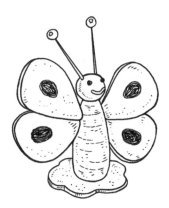

- Apple slices
- Carrot
- Grape
- Raisins
- Cranberries

- Frosting tube
- Cloves
- Watermelon slice
- Toothpicks

Make wings out of apple slices. Attach wings to carrot-body with cut toothpicks, and then attach a grape for the head. Decorate the wings with raisins, attaching with dabs of frosting or cut toothpicks. Use cloves for eyes. Draw a mouth with frosting tube. Add toothpicks topped with cranberries for antennae. Create a base using a slice or chunk of watermelon. Attach butterfly to base with toothpicks.

CRAWLY CRAB

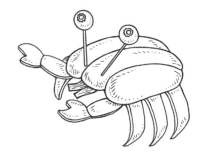

- Red pepper
- Grapes and cloves,
  or olives with pimentos
- Toothpicks

Cut pepper in half length-wise to form body. Slice the other half of the pepper to form six legs and two claws. Attach parts with tooth-picks. Use toothpicks topped with either grapes and cloves or olives with pimentos to form eye stalks.

Printmaking

This lettering style is Open Face Schoolbell.

From potatoes to pie tins, apples to erasers, broccoli to bottles, your grandkids will find all kinds of surprising patterns that can be made by dipping in paint and then pressing on paper. That's printmaking!

Note: Grandma needs to do the cutting on all projects requiring a knife.

On a potato or apple half, have your grandchild draw a simple design. Make ¼" cuts to mark the outline of the design.

Carefully cut around the design, and there's your print block!

Dip into a bowl of tempera paint or other water-based paint and print onto heavy paper or poster board.

To add different layers of patterns, trim down the original print block and use different colors to give your butterfly multi-colored wings.

Another way to make a stamp –

On a piece of thick cardboard, trace a shape you like. Cut it out. Glue on a chunk of a sponge, a thread spool, or other object for a handle.

Make a patriotic sign or banner with star print blocks in red, white, and blue.

Repeat designs to make frames, picnic placemats, holiday banners.

What can you find outside or around the house to make fun prints? Look for things with interesting shapes and textures.

Leaves, sponges, rags, yarn, sticks, kitchen utensils – just about anything can be used to create interesting designs, shapes, and patterns.

A broccoli floret cut in half makes an amazing tree! Just dip in paint, press onto paper. Add other details to make a forest.

Fill a barnyard with baby chicks using cotton balls dipped in yellow paint. Add a few lines for definition and black dots for eyes.

These flowers are prints of the bottom of a water bottle. Draw stems and leaves to complete the bottle impression.

Here's another way to make a print design!

Turn a pie pan upside down and cover with paint.

Use a brush, cotton swab, or other tool to draw your design in the paint.

Place a sheet of paper over the pie pan.

Carefully peel off the sheet for a perfect print!

PRINTING BY HAND

Most people start their journey in art with finger painting. Explore ways your grandkids can have fun with hand-made art! This might get messy, but the grandkids will love it!

FRIEND POSTER

Celebrate your circle of family, friends, teammates, etc. Set out bowls of different colored water-based or child safe craft paints. Have each person dip their hand in and press onto heavy paper. Sign with a name, message or design. Kids can enjoy hanging on a door or wall to remember a special time.

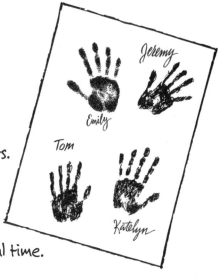

HANDY TREE

You can make a tree by first placing your flattened hand in a pie pan of brown paint then printing a tree "trunk".

Add colorful leaves by cutting small pieces of colored paper or stamping different colors with the eraser of a pencil...red apples or pink blossoms, for example.

SPECIAL SIGNATURE

Use the "signature" of your handprint to make a special card.

Put your handprint on a piece of card stock.

always hold my hand

Cut out a heart or other design and add your message. Glue to the palm of the handprint.

FLOWER GARDEN

Start with a large sheet of paper.

Place your hand in a shallow dish of paint then press onto paper in a circular pattern to create the petals of your flowers.

Use your fingers to "brush" a contrasting center to your flower.

Use your fingers as a paint brush and add stems and leaves to your flower garden.

FINGERTIP ART

Just press a finger into paint then see what you can create when you press onto paper. Let your imagination go!

The possibilities are endless!

Make layers of prints in different colors for scales or feathers.

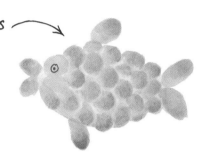

What images can you imagine when you add pencil or marker details to a finger print?

Make simple hand print animals, adding cut paper for eyes, ears, mouths, etc.

This border was made with a fork!

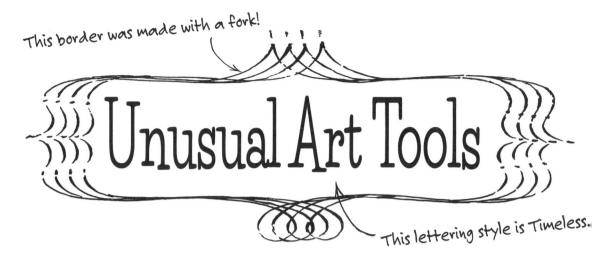

Unusual Art Tools

This lettering style is Timeless.

Look around...unusual art tools are everywhere! An "Unusual Art Tools Treasure Hunt" can help you brainstorm and think creatively together.

Just about anything can become a paint brush...

...consider the possibilities.

Use cups, glasses, and containers of various sizes to make shapes...

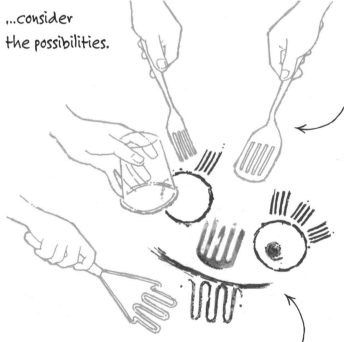

...combine with a potato masher, slotted spoon, or fork for added effect. What else can you find in the kitchen drawer?

Create faces, creatures, or fun abstract designs.

Dip tea bags in different paint colors to create interesting textured patterns.

Pick a toy truck that has a patterned tread on its wheels. Try different colors after each one dries to create a colorful abstract!

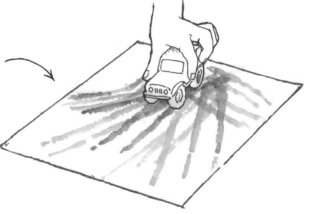

A bundle of uncooked pasta can be used to create fun and unusual line work.

Experiment by combining more than one technique to create a uniquely personal masterpiece!

Cut a sponge into shapes that can be dipped into paint. Press the heart shape sponge into a flower petal pattern.

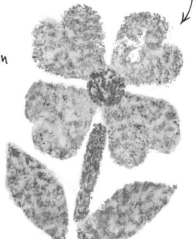

Make a whole garden of flowers with a combination of shapes and colors...

...or butterflies...

...or bunnies.

No paint brush? No problem...

Make your own from a clothespin and just about anything you can think of. A piece of sponge, yarn, cottonball, bubblewrap, or even spinach leaves.

Enjoy a sunny day outside with these fun (and messy!) ideas.

Clip sheets of paper to a clothesline, or attach to a chain link fence.

Fill several small spray bottles or water toys with diluted watercolors, and let the kids have at it!

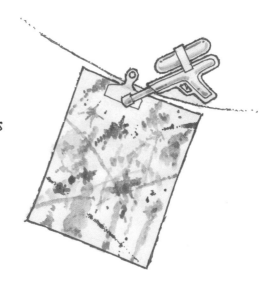

Make a paint ball with a kitchen sponge...

...cut the sponge into 8 to 10 strips...

...and tie together with string, floss, twist tie, or a rubber band.

Lay a large piece of paper on the ground and see what fun designs appear when you toss the paint-dipped sponge ball. SPLAT!

UNUSUAL TOOLS A TO Z

Once kids get the idea of using ordinary things around the house for unusual art tools, they'll have a blast thinking creatively. Paint a texture, dip a shape into paint, or make your own unique paintbrush and handle. Here are over 50 things to get your imagination flowing:

- Asparagus (use tip or end for different effects)

- Bottle cap

- Bolt

- Bubble wrap (wrap around a paper towel tube, paint, and roll out a cool spotted texture)

- Cardboard tubes (toilet paper, paper towels)

- Celery stalks and leaves

- Coil or spring, from an old spiral notebook, makes a cool spiral texture when painted and rolled across a page

- Comb

- Cookie cutter

- Corks from bottles

- Dowel, wooden or plastic

- Eyedropper

- Feather

- Flower

- Foam or sponge ball on a craft stick handle

- Foil, crumpled

- Fork

- Game pieces or markers

- Hands and fingers

- Herbs bundled in a rubber band

- Interconnecting toy pieces

- Jewelry, leftover plastic or costume pieces

- Knife (plastic), and other plastic ware pieces

- Lace

- Leaves

- Make-up applicator

- Marshmallow

- Noodles, such as penne, form circles by dipping end in paint; or bow-tie makes unique shape

- Orange peel

- Pencil eraser

- Playing cards, make thin straight lines by dipping edge in paint and impressing lightly on paper

- Puzzle pieces, from a puzzle with missing pieces

- Q-tip cotton swabs

- Rolling pin, wrapped in yarn, rubber bands, bubble wrap and other textures

- Rubber snakes, spiders and bugs

- Spaghetti bundle, uncooked

- Sponge, with a clothes pin handle

- Straw

- Toy car tracks

- Toothpicks

- Toothbrush

- Utensils (all kinds from the kitchen drawer)

- Vegetables, cut into spears or shapes

- Washers from the tool chest make circular shapes

- Weeds, bundled with rubber band on a stick handle

- Yarn, bundle short lengths, secure with rubber band around the end of a dowel

- Zip-top bag, snip a hole to make a squeezy paint dispenser

- Zoo animals and plastic toys

Hand Lettering*

Open the world of beautiful hand lettering for your grand-children! There are many examples in this section While younger children may want to trace the letters shown, older children may prefer to embellish, improvise, or even create their own alphabet.

Here are a few pointers to get started…

Fine-, medium-, and heavy-tipped felt pens create different line thicknesses, as well as paint brushes of various sizes and calligraphy pens (beginner sets can be found at most craft stores).

After selecting the word or words you want to letter, choose a compatible lettering style, one that reflects the mood of the text.

Is the mood thoughtful or whimsical? Fun or formal? Comic, cute, or classic?

- If you're working with a message or a quotation, which words are to be emphasized? How do you see them emphasized?

- What about line breaks? Does the layout look good, as well as fit into the space?

- How do you want to treat "empty" space, such as background, frame, or margins?

Here are a couple of ideas to keep in mind when you create your own personal masterpiece. Start with a rough idea sketched on scratch paper. Experiment with various letter styles and sizes until you come up with one that fits both the text and the space. Try different layout approaches. When you've chosen a favorite layout, rough it out using the true measurements of the finished piece. Use light lines that you easily can erase later.

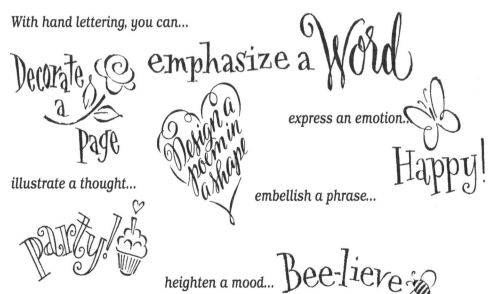

this is hand lettering

this is hand lettering

AND THIS IS HAND LETTERING

With hand lettering, you can...

Decorate a Page

emphasize a Word

express an emotion...

Design a poem in a shape

Happy!

illustrate a thought...

embellish a phrase...

party!

heighten a mood... Bee-lieve

SIMPLE STACKING LAYOUT

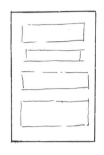

FOLLOW YOUR *dreams!* ANYTHING IS *possible*

Sometimes the simplest solution is the best, as with this example of stacked words or phrased. This keeps the message clear and easy-to-read.

ASYMMETRICAL LAYOUT

Throw things off-center a bit for an attention-grabbing composition. Slant lines, tilt words, and vary size. In this example, the line at the bottom provides a foundation.

Good FRIENDS *are the family we chose for ourselves*

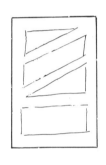

FITTING IT ALL IN LAYOUT

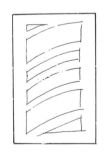

THE SOUND *of laughter is* MUSIC *for the soul*

Emphasize only the most important words by using larger type than used for the rest of the text. Put the words in an arc, curve, or slant so they will fit comfortably on the page. Script lettering (letters joined in a continuous line) helps save space.

The following pages are examples of hand lettering styles.
Trace or use them for inspiration—Or create your own!

Open Face Schoolbell

Aa Bb Cc Dd Ee
Ff Gg Hh Ii Jj Kk
Ll Mm Nn Oo Pp
Qq Rr Ss Tt Uu
Vv Ww Xx Yy Zz

Giggle

Aa Bb Cc Dd Ee
Ff Gg Hh Ii Jj Kk
Ll Mm Nn Oo Pp
Qq Rr Ss Tt Uu
Vv Ww Xx Yy Zz

Easy Peasy

Aa Bb Cc Dd Ee
Ff Gg Hh Ii Jj Kk
Ll Mm Nn Oo Pp
Qq Rr Ss Tt Uu
Vv Ww Xx Yy Zz

Ladybug

Aa Bb Cc Dd Ee
Ff Gg Hh Ii Jj
Kk Ll Mm Nn
Oo Pp Qq Rr Ss
Tt Uu Vv Ww Xx
Yy Zz

Timeless

Aa Bb Cc Dd Ee

Ff Gg Hh Ii Jj Kk

Ll Mm Nn Oo Pp

Qq Rr Ss Tt Uu

Vv Ww Xx Yy Zz

Make it more special with personalized hand lettering.
What ideas can you dream up? Here are some starters:

Personalized Message Signs

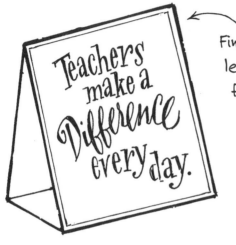

Find a meaningful phrase and
letter it on a tent-card you
fold from card stock to set on
a desk, or attach a message
to heavy foam core to hang
on a wall.

Celebration sign

Celebrate in a big way by making
a decoration to hang on a wall—
Or leave as an outdoor surpise.
Just attach your sign to a
box with a heavy rock in it
so it doesn't fly away.

Highlight the
name in a
special way!

Memory-Makers

Start with an inexpensive plain photo sleeve album, scrapbook, or notebook. Personalize a design on paper and attach to the front cover, for your own special memories or to give as a gift.

Name it & Claim it!

Create your own recognizable name label or logo to personalize your things.

Greeting Cards & Notes

Show you put extra care into your special card to say Happy Birthday, Thank You, You're Invited...Add designs, doodles, or additions like ribbon, lace or paper cut-outs.

Posters & Wall art!

Use a variety of type styles to express the different thoughts.

Open spaces are an opportunity for you to have fun with decorative design.

DOODLE & DECORATE A SAYING

Create a frame like this with markers or gel pens. First, letter a phrase that inspires you, then doodle a border however you like. Hang it on a wall, tape in a locker or make an encouraging statement to give to someone.

This lettering style is Timeless, set in all capitals.

YOUR NAME, YOUR STYLE

Motivate, encourage, and inspire grandkids to feel good about being the special people they are with unique-to-them personal expressions.

YOUR NAME BOARD

Cut out the letters of your name. Make them big!

Use construction paper, gift wrap, fabric, foil, wallpaper...

...or use plain paper and paint your own design on each letter.

Glue letters onto a large board.

Add drawings, pictures, photos, or cut shapes that stand for all the things you love!

VISION BOARD

Join your grandkids in creating a personal vision board! No matter how old or how young we are, it's easy to lose sight of our goals, our hopes for the future, and what we need to do to make our dreams come true.

So what's a vision board? It starts with a plain poster board for each person, along with a stack of magazines. Everyone goes through the magazines page by page, clipping out pictures, words, and captions that reflect interests and spark the imagination.

But magazine pictures don't tell the whole story of "you." Include drawings, artwork, photos, and printouts from the internet.

Now arrange your words and images on your poster board...perhaps you might want to put your favorite photo of yourself in the middle! While you're working, talk about your grandkids' goals and dreams. Suggest ways to make these things happen...encourage realistic plans...clear thinking... flexibility...optimism. Give your grandkids the benefit of your knowledge, experience, and insight. And what better way to model positive aging and lifelong learning than with your own vision board?

When satisfied with the board, attach items with glue or tape. Suggest that each person display the board where it will be seen every day...or, if someone would rather keep it private, the board could be slid under the bed or kept in the closet. Just remember to bring it out frequently and spend time with it!

WORDS TO INSPIRE

A word or phrase that inspires can motivate, encourage, or warm a heart. On card stock or poster board, glue cut-out or drawn and decorated letters. See how words and images work to create a mood. Send to a friend...stand it up on a desk...attach a ribbon and hang it from your room door.

CREST

Create a personal crest to show your achievements and interests. Use either clay or board for this one. Decide on the crest's size and shape. Divide it into as many sections as you want, school, club, sport, special interest, band or group name.
Create your own border treatment and decorative designs.
Most important – your name!

Do a search on the internet together and see if you can find your family's name crest. It's interesting to kids and they may want to use the design as inspiration.

LIFE SIZE SELF PORTRAIT

This is great fun for all, but you need a big sheet of paper, such as newsprint, and enough room to move around! Have each grandchild strike a pose in front of a lamp so his or her shadow falls on the paper. Draw around the silhouette, and then let the "poser" fill in at will! You can do this as a sidewalk chalk activity, too!

PHOTO PORTRAIT

Start with a clear photo portrait.

Cover half the face with paper and tape down. Finish the other side of the face with pencil, pen, charcoal, or crayon.

Kids can complete their portrait as realistically as possible— or make it as creative and far out as they want. Half person-half monster? Or lion? Or...?

Try "bouncing" the letters to add interest.

Frames, Jewelry, and Gifts

Handmade gifts are the best gifts of all!

KEEPSAKE FRAMES

Buy a plain photo frame or mat frame at a hobby or discount store, and then personalize it!

Glue on fancy buttons, silk flowers, cut paper shapes, or draw a design with markers or paint.

Frame your own artwork or a handwritten thought for someone special.

See how a simple frame or mat can become a treasured keepsake!

Best Mom Ever!

Add your own decorations from cut paper.

Create a souvenir of a special event or vacation by framing concert tickets, theme park passes, brochure cover, map, photo, or other print mementos.

Embellish the frame with related colors and designs, or found objects.

Make a fabric background with either one piece of fabric, or a collage of colorful scraps.

Cut a shape out of construction paper...

...star, heart, flower...

Best Friends Forever

...add your message, and then glue onto your background.

JEWELRY AND MAGNETS

Create unique gifts with items you have around the house. Keep your eyes open for things that might be repurposed into fun magnets and jewelry.

Cut a small piece of 1/8" thick black foam core.

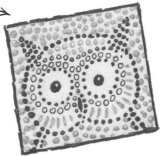

Decorate with gel, foam, or glitter pens...colored pencils...cut paper...fabric scraps...button...shell.

Your design could be a favorite animal, a classic pattern, or abstract shapes.

Glue on a pin back or magnet that can be purchased at craft stores.

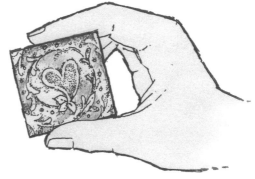

Create unique pieces of jewelry or gifts with items you have around the house.

Decorate bottlecaps...

Glue them to foam core and add a magnet to the back.

Make whatever message you want! DAD, FRIEND, Pet's Name, etc.

Paint pasta in bright patterns, trendy zebra or leopard print...

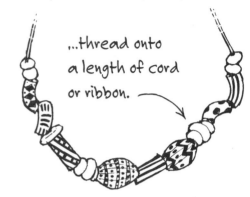

...thread onto a length of cord or ribbon.

Here's a way to recycle bottle caps!

On card stock, trace around the cap. Paint or draw a design in the circle, and then carefully cut out the circle.

Glue design onto the top of the cap, or in the inside...or both.

Grandma, punch a small hole in the rim. (You can use a nail and a hammer).

Cut a length of cord or ribbon for a pendant, or attach to a lanyard.

Fingernail polish can turn a plain metal washer into a bright and colorful pendant!

Attach to cord, ribbon, or lanyard.

WOVEN BRACELET

Use bright gum or candy wrappers to make a colorful weave!

Metallics work well, too, such as inner lining of chewing gum sticks.

You could also make your own design or pattern on a sheet of plain paper.

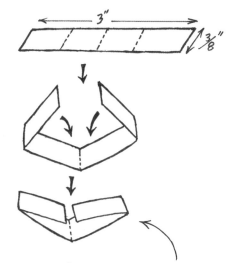

Fold strips in quarters, as shown.

Repeat the steps above for multiple bracelet "links."

Then begin to connect them as shown.

Weave pieces together until desired length.

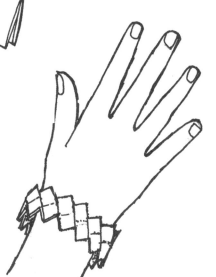

77

WEAVE A WONDERFUL GIFT

This image shows the basic directions for weaving. Note how the first strip goes over then under; the strip beside it is woven in the opposite way, starting by going under, then over the next; and so on, to create this checkerboard-like effect. One helpful tip for kids is to lay a strip of double sided tape across the top of a foam core piece, and carefully lay down the alternating colors of paper, adhering the top of each strip to the tape. Now do the same thing by adhering a strip of double sided tape vertically down the left side of the foam core. To this, lay down alternating color paper strips, each one attached to the tape on the left end. Grandma should check the layout before the child tapes anything down. With the paper strips secured in place, the child can more easily weave without losing track of the paper strips. Caution them to be gentle so the paper doesn't tear.

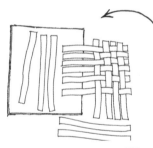

Cut a piece of foam core or heavy backer board. Cut strips of construction paper, decorative paper, or fabric. Weave strips together to desired size. Glue or tape to the foam core for a decorative design.

From another piece of foam core or mat board, cut out a shape for the weaving to show through, and add a message.

Attach the two pieces together with tape, glue or tie a cord through punched holes. Attach a backing on it for standing or hanging.

I love Nana

This typeface is Ladybug.

Get Outdoors

Explore a rainbow of ideas for outdoor creations!

Take the grands for a walk around your yard and neighborhood. As you're spotting the "tools" for these projects, you're teaching the youngsters to observe and appreciate the many little gifts of nature.

Hint: Have a big bucket of sidewalk chalk ready so kids can go outside and create any time!

PAINT WITH NATURE

Find a few natural paintbrushes – it could be just about anything! Cattail, Fern, Flower, Leaf, or Feather.

Dip your paintbrush in a shallow bowl of paint...

...and gently press it onto the paper and carefully lift off to leave an impression.

For a layered effect, apply a light watercolor wash to the paper and let it dry before painting.

Make an impression of a daisy!

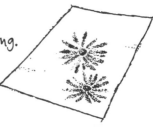

PAINTED ROCKS

Look for small, smooth rocks that inspire your art.
Before using, wash them and let them dry completely.

Use acrylic paint to create your artwork.

(Remember, acrylic paints are not washable,
so cover clothing and work surfaces when working
with it.) Have a variety of brush sizes available.

You could make a "gift rock"...

...or the shape of your rock might remind you of
an animal,...

...or little ladybug.

You might have found a heart-shaped rock,...

...or a perfect oval for an owl.

Let imaginations run wild!

Once dry, rocks can be added to a flower pot, lined up on a shelf,
given to a friend, or...how about this? Leave it someplace outside as a
happy surprise for someone to find. Imagine how you would feel if you
picked up a rock with a saying, such as, You are Awesome!...You are
Beautiful!...Smile...Dream!

NATURE COLLAGE

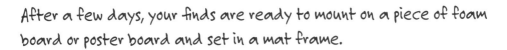

Find interesting flowers
and leaves for a nature collage.

Flatten your finds by laying them
between two pieces of waxed paper.
Slip them inside a heavy book, or put them under a heavy item.

After a few days, your finds are ready to mount on a piece of foam
board or poster board and set in a mat frame.

A shadow box frame allows you to add a few 3-D objects, such as
pebbles, pods, or small rocks.

TERRA COTTA DECOR

Plain terra cotta pots can be
painted with acrylics to brighten
the porch, patio, or garden.

Plant a few flower seeds in soil in
your pot and watch your plant sprout and bloom!

(Remember, acrylic paints are not washable, so cover clothing and
work surfaces when working with it.)

LEAF PAINTING

Gather a collection of interesting
leaves from various trees and shrubs
around your yard and neighborhood.

Make an impression...

Dip your leaf in a shallow bowl of paint.

Gently press the leaf onto a piece of paper, and then carefully lift
off.

Make a leaf print...

Several impressions of one leaf...

...or several leaves...

...in different colors make an interesting composition.

Use a spray bottle...

Fill one or several small spray bottles
with diluted paint.

Place leaf onto a piece of paper.

Spray over the leaf.

Carefully remove the leaf to leave a colorful negative impression!

This type was done with a big, fat marker!

TAPE and STRINGS... and ALL KINDS OF THINGS

Here's an easy, fun, and fascinating technique for kids of all ages to enjoy!

PULLED STRING PAINTING

Simple string, paper, and paint combine for amazing art!

You'll need:
• Paper   • String or yarn   • Tempera or activity paint
• Small containers for paint cups

Fill the cups with paint, and have kids coat the string or yarn by dipping it into a paint cup. Kids lay the strings anywhere on the paper and drag, swirl, or wiggle the string all around to create the artwork. Use lots of different colors and mix them up on the paper with various strings. (Let each color dry before adding another or the painting may turn muddy brown.)

• Kids can use various lengths of string to create circles and swirls.

• Have kids fold the paper in half and pull several strings through in any direction. Open the paper to reveal the creation!

More ways to use your string masterpiece!

While the paint is still wet, add texture by pressing into it using a cotton ball, sponge, paintbrush – even a toy car! Experiment with the textures created by different objects.

After the paint is dry, kids can cut the string art into fun shapes such as leaves, hearts, stars, people, etc. Use these cut outs to make a collage by gluing onto heavy paper or another art piece.

Use string art designs to make fun borders for framing pictures of family and friends.

SPRAY PAINT STRING ART

Lay lengths of string across a sheet of paper,...

...tape down ends.

Spray with diluted paint and let dry,...

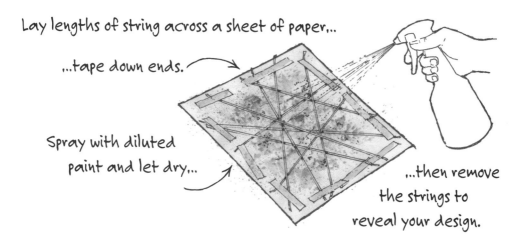

...then remove the strings to reveal your design.

STRING ART TEXTURES AND PATTERNS

Tightly wrap a length of yarn around a rolling pin. Explore creative ways to wrap the yarn!

Make a tray out of aluminum foil that's as wide as the rolling pin. Use this as a "paint bucket" to apply the paint to the roller.

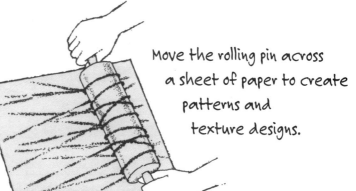

Move the rolling pin across a sheet of paper to create patterns and texture designs.

Bonus – When the yarn is removed from the rolling pin, you will have a multicolored length of string to use as a hanger for your project!

RESIST

Kids won't be able to resist these fun projects! Salt, tape, crayons are just a few tools to make "Resist" Art. Lay any of these on paper, brush over with paint, and the paint will not adhere, leaving a really cool effect! Create a world of wild, funky, and fun designs and patterns. Here are a few examples, but you and your grandkids will come up with many more ideas!

SALT & TAPE RESIST

SALT RESIST: Apply a layer of watercolor wash over a sheet of paper. While paint is still wet, sprinkle table salt across the surface and watch as a crystalline pattern appears!

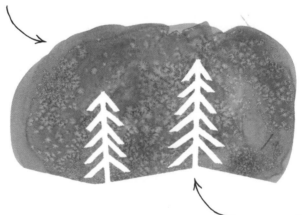

TAPE RESIST: Before you do a salt resist, apply masking tape to a plain surface, creating a picture or pattern, such as the trees in the example. Paint across the whole area, including covering the tape and sprinkle salt across all. When completely dry, peel off the tape and see the design left behind.

BLACK GLUE RESIST

Make your drawing with black glue. You can purchase black glue in craft stores or make your own by mixing black craft paint into regular glue.

When the glue is dry, color over with paint, ink, or colored pencils. The glue will not absorb the color, and the result is a dramatic effect something like stained glass leading.

CRAYON RESIST

Make a line drawing with crayons...

...then brush a coat of paint over it...

...your crayon drawing will reappear!

Abstract & Geometrics

Drawing isn't all about realistic pictures. Shapes, patterns, colors, and textures working together can create a mood, convey a feeling, or simply delight the eye!

DRIP PAINT ART

Here's a way to get outdoors and create abstract art, too!

Hang large sheets of paper from a clothesline or piece of string stretched between two patio chairs. Fill several small squeeze bottles or old shampoo bottles with various colors of paint.

Squeeze paint and let the paint drip down the page.

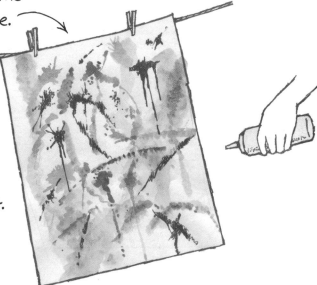

Layer colors...

...let one layer dry, then add another.

...turn the paper on its side...

...start another layer of paint.

...experiment with colors and have fun!

MONTAGE OF SHAPES

Using one shape or several, you can create an interesting montage.

Trace around different shaped objects found in the junk drawer or on a desk. Overlap the traced shapes. See the example below for the idea. Next, color in the different shapes formed. You can see the results on the cover of the book.

Any object will work to trace around!

This was done with just a ruler and a sheet of paper!

Using circular objects will give you an altogether different abstract design. Trace around jar lids, plates, drinking glasses, small bottles, etc... Try using shading when you color them in. Using chalk or chalk pastels you can gently rub the colors together. For a simple monochromatic look.

Use charcoals or pencils and see how the different shading creates values of light to dark grey.

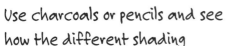

You don't have to trace around objects for this color-in-the-shape idea. Just take your time and draw a "Scribble" with intersecting lines, then color in the shapes. (If you're ever waiting in a restaurant that provides crayons at the table this is a fun art project to have at the ready.)

SWINGING BOTTLE DESIGNS

Use a squirt bottle with lid, such as a condiment bottle, hair color applicator, or a plastic water bottle with small hole punched in the lid. You can do this outdoors by hanging the bottle with string from a branch. Place a large piece of paper or an old sheet as your canvas on the ground.

Fill the bottle with paint that is about the consistency of milk. Suspend it so the dispenser end will face down, with your paper canvas below. Remove lid, give the bottle a little nudge, and allow the swinging bottle to dispense paint onto the paper. Create different designs by moving the bottle to swing in a circular motion, and back and forth. Fill different bottles with a variety of colors to make a vibrant abstract creation.

Hint: if paint does not dispense, poke a small hole in the other end of the bottle to dispense air. You might also need to dilute it a little to make it the right consistency.

EYE DROPPER ABSTRACTS

Fill an eye dropper with paint...

Set out little cups with different paint color in each.

...squirt small dots wherever you like on a sheet of paper.

Try adding more colors. You may even want to layer or overlap your dots or dab one color over another.

PAPER SCRAP ABSTRACTS

Make a scrappy design of any kind, or create a scrappy background for a central figure. Cut a pile of shapes of various sizes (1/2" - 2" chunks) and colors from construction paper, magazine pages, gift wrap, or greeting card covers. Separate pieces by color, each color family being in a separate pile or on a paper plate.

Younger grandkids might find larger shapes easier to work with, while older grandkids may be ready to work with very small pieces.

Then, with glue, create your paper scrap design.

SCRAPPY FISH

Here's an idea for a fish in a sea of scraps!

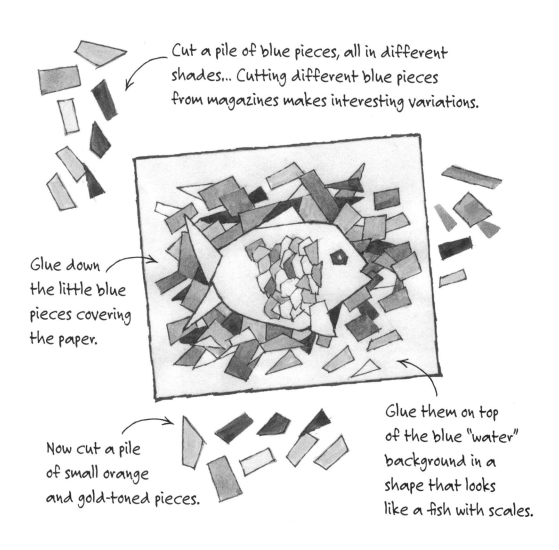

Cut a pile of blue pieces, all in different shades... Cutting different blue pieces from magazines makes interesting variations.

Glue down the little blue pieces covering the paper.

Now cut a pile of small orange and gold-toned pieces.

Glue them on top of the blue "water" background in a shape that looks like a fish with scales.

What other themes can you imagine? An airplane in the sky? A bird in a tree? A turtle in sand?

MAKING ART WITH MATH

Every child is unique, and some will enjoy the free-form ideas in this book while others will gravitate toward more linear projects like the ones in this section using ruled lines, addition, division, and more. Self-expression, a feeling of accomplishment, and fun—especially, FUN—are the goals!

SPINNER

Use simple math concepts to make a colorful spinner! All you need is card stock, string, and a selection of crayons, markers, or colored pencils.

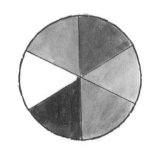

On cardstock, draw a circle, either by tracing around a circular item or using a compass. Carefully cut out the circle. Mark the center, and then divide it into six equal segments. Color each segment as desired.

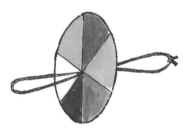

Now punch two holes 1/2"apart at the center of the circle.

Measure 36" of string, thread it through the center holes so the string is halved – tie a knot in the loose ends, positioning the circle at the center of the two halves.

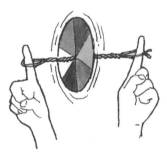

Flip the circle repeatedly until the string is twisted on both ends. Pull the ends and watch the colors mix! – Move your fingers in and out and keep the spinner spinning!

ORIGAMI

Origami is the art of folding paper into shapes to create an object or animal, etc. Here's one example of a Cool Cat!

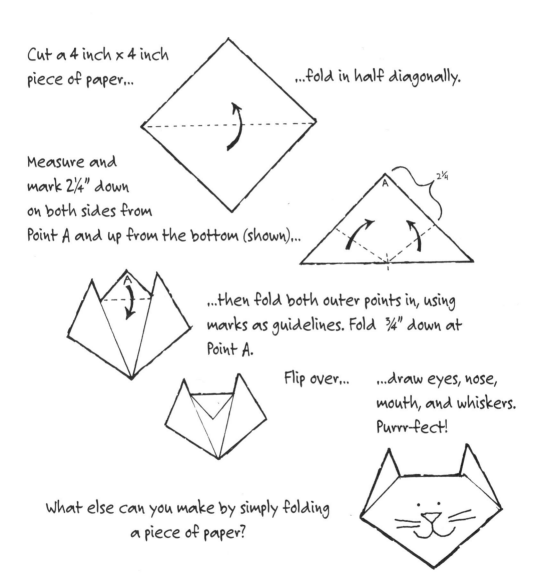

Cut a 4 inch x 4 inch piece of paper...

...fold in half diagonally.

Measure and mark 2¼" down on both sides from Point A and up from the bottom (shown)...

...then fold both outer points in, using marks as guidelines. Fold ¾" down at Point A.

Flip over...

...draw eyes, nose, mouth, and whiskers. Purrr-fect!

What else can you make by simply folding a piece of paper?

RELAXATION WHEEL

For this artistic idea, grandkids can make precise measurements with a compass and ruler...or they can estimate their measurements using a straightline tool (ruler, side of an envelope or note pad, etc) and round objects of different sizes to trace around (spool of thread, jar lid, juice glass, plate, etc).

Cut a square piece of paper. An 8″ square is easy to cut from a regular letter-sized paper.

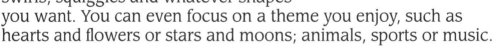

Determine the very center of the paper and put a pencil dot there. Next, either with the compass or circular objects, draw circles from that inner point in increasing sizes. You can also use your straight-edge or ruler to make equally spaced lines radiating from the center out. Let your imagination go, and with fine line markers, fill in the spaces with details, swirls, squiggles and whatever shapes you want. You can even focus on a theme you enjoy, such as hearts and flowers or stars and moons; animals, sports or music.

The practice of coloring is said to be a calming activity. So encourage your grandkids to take their time and let their minds relax as they fill in these repeated patterns and images with markers or colored pencils.

Through the projects in this book, your grandkids have experienced creativity, problem-solving, patience and self-reflection.
Enjoy special times together and watch their imaginations soar!